A Pup in the Dry Plains

Written by Heather Horn

Illustrated by Victoria Skakandi

© 2024 The Good and the Beautiful, LLC
goodandbeautiful.com
Cover design by Phillip Colhouer

Challenge Words

groups

hyena

Kalahari Desert

learn

scorpion

CHAPTER 1
A Dry Place

Long, long ago, giant lakes and rivers spread across the tip of Africa.

But after years and years of hot, blistering sun and very little rain, the land has been baked dry. This is the Kalahari Desert.

Kalahari means "the great thirst." The land is hot and thirsty, and the animals are too. Tall sand dunes surround the flat, dry plains.

It is the dry season. The last of the water holes are drying up fast. All the animals have a hard time finding shade in the open, sandy land.

Many of the large herd animals, such as zebra and buffalo, move north each year, looking for flowing rivers.

For those that stay behind, life in the Kalahari is harsh! Tall giraffes and gray elephants search for leaves on the few trees and plants that grow here.

The trees have deep roots that make them strong. They have to be in order to survive here.

The best place to stay cool is in the shade of one of these trees. It is where big cats take long naps in the afternoons.

Some of the smaller animals know another place to stay cool.

They hide deep in holes in the sand. Some holes are small, and some are wide.

Up pops a little head from one.

This is Gus. He is a meerkat, and he lives in this burrow with his family.

In spite of their name, meerkats are not cats! They are part of the mongoose family. Meerkats are small, but they know how to stay safe from the many dangers in the Kalahari.

CHAPTER 2
Welcome, Pups

Meerkat families live together in larger groups called mobs. There are twenty meerkats in Gus's mob.

Gus has a very big job today. It is his turn to serve as the lookout for the mob. He is a new big brother.

His mother gave birth to four new pups one month ago. Today, the pups will see outside their dark burrow for the first time.

Gus stands almost a foot tall on his hind legs. He leans on his long tail, using it like a kickstand on a bike. Black rings around Gus's eyes are like sunglasses that help him see better in the bright sun.

He scans the wide sky for eagles and looks across the flat plains for hyenas, snakes, and other sneaky animals. If he sees danger, it is his job to alert the mob.

Gus sees that it is safe, so he calls inside the burrow for the pups to come out.

Gus's parents, Penny and Hank, lead their little pups out of the burrow. Roxy, Rex, Lola, and Chase take their first clumsy steps outside.

Chase is the last one out, but he boldly explores this new place. Gus keeps a close eye on Chase.

There is not much food by the burrow. Penny and Hank will go find food. They will need to be careful. There is a lot of danger across the dry land. They must stick together to stay safe. Penny and Hank will return before sundown.

Gus is left to babysit the four new pups while another meerkat takes a turn as lookout.

Oh boy, does Gus have his hands full! Roxy rolls over the top of Rex, and Chase tugs on Lola. The siblings have lots to learn.

CHAPTER 3
The First Lesson

Older meerkats such as Gus teach the young pups while their parents are out hunting during the day.

God gave meerkats skills for living in the hot sand. Gus is only a year old, but he knows the skills Chase will need to learn over the next few months. Gus will be Chase's teacher. Their siblings have teachers too.

The first lesson Chase must learn is how to put his digging skills to good use. Their burrow has many openings and many rooms.

Deep in the sand are tunnels that lead to rooms for sleeping and rooms for waste. There are also holes and tunnels for fast escapes.

Gus teaches Chase how to dig a wide bolt hole. It is used as a fast escape in case of danger. Gus begins digging the hole with his sharp, curved claws. Sand goes flying as Chase looks on from behind.

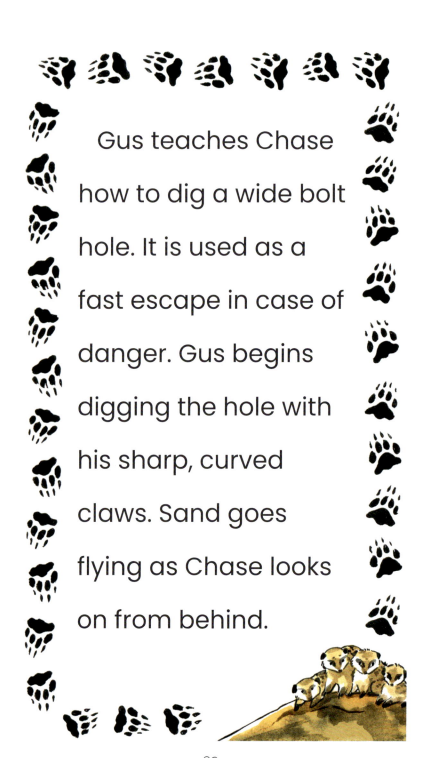

Chase closes his ears to keep the flying sand out. Lenses on his eyes push away the sand like wipers wiping away the rain on a car window.

Sometimes meerkats share their burrows with other animals, such as these little critters. This saves time digging and gives all of them more places to escape danger.

CHAPTER 4
Stay Alert

While the helper meerkats are busy teaching the young pups, the rest of the mob take turns as lookouts.

It is time for Gus to teach Chase how to hunt. Meerkats like to eat bugs, grubs, scorpions, and snakes!

Some snakes and all scorpions have venom. Most animals that get bitten or stung will get very sick, but not meerkats.

Chase sniffs and digs as a scorpion scoots across the sand. He bats at the scorpion as she wiggles her eight legs. Chase doesn't know how to trap her, so she gets away.

Gus shows Chase how to flip the scorpion and remove the stinger. Chase tries again and traps the scorpion.

Danger! The lookout meerkat sees a hyena coming too close to the burrow, and he barks to alert the others.

All the meerkats freeze and stand tall on their hind legs. They look left and right. Then they run for the nearest hole.

Oh no! Here comes the hyena now. The hair on his back stands on end as he sniffs closer and closer.

The brothers are too far from the burrow. Gus alerts Chase. Chase drops his dinner and dashes for the bolt hole. The hyena goes after them.

They duck into the bolt hole just in time. The hyena sticks his nose inside the hole, but he cannot reach them. He digs with his front paws, but he still can't reach them. The hyena gives up and goes home.

CHAPTER 5
In the Old Tree

A lonely old shepherd's tree offers shade. In its branches is a ten-foot-wide weaver nest.

This weaver bird apartment is almost one hundred years old, and more than one hundred weaver bird families live here. The little brown birds dart in and out of the holes at the bottom of the nest.

The little weavers must be careful. A yellow cape cobra slithers up the tree and sneaks into the nest while the birds are away for the day. He likes to snack on eggs.

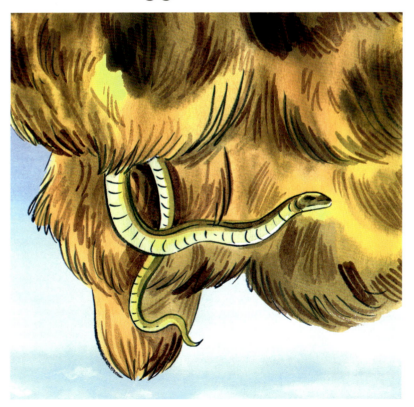

Chase, Gus, and the rest of the mob that lives by the old tree must be careful too. Cobras like to eat eggs up in the nest, but they also slither along the sand, looking for more to eat.

Sometimes the snake follows the meerkats deep into the burrow, but the mob knows the maze of tunnels well and is able to hide from the snake.

The mob is busy hunting in the midday sun. Their light tan fur and dark stripes help them blend in to make them harder to spot. The new pups are getting very good at finding bugs and trapping scorpions.

Yikes! The lookout meerkat sees the yellow cobra coming.

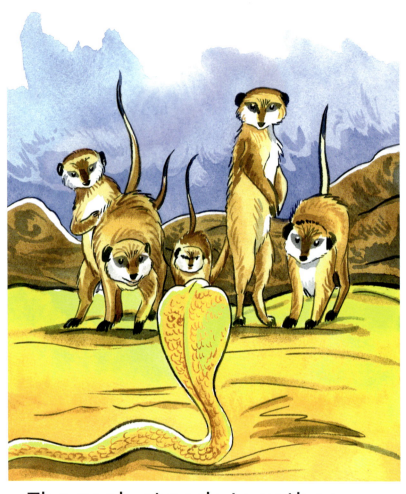

The mob stands together to look big and mean. They chatter and make lots of noise to drive the snake away.

CHAPTER 6
The Thirsty Land

The Kalahari waits for rain. Big dark clouds roll in, forming a thunderhead in the west.

Lightning flashes, and thunder booms, but no rain falls on the thirsty land.

Meerkats don't need much water. They get their water from the bugs they eat.

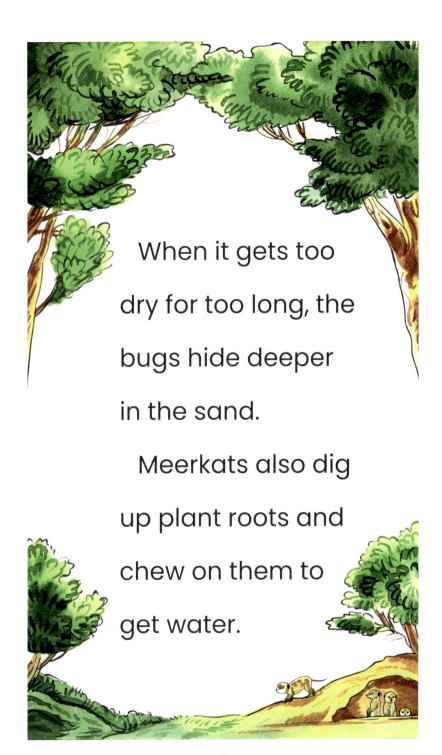

When it gets too dry for too long, the bugs hide deeper in the sand. Meerkats also dig up plant roots and chew on them to get water.

The big sky has been dark and cloudy for days, but still, no rain has fallen. All the animals need rain soon. Food is getting harder and harder to find, and some animals will not survive to the next season without rain.

Chase is getting bolder. He explores farther away from the burrow. Gus always keeps a close eye on him, but today, Chase roams a little too far from the mob.

Chase follows the tiny tracks of a scorpion until the tracks stop by a big stone. Where did it go?

Chase stands tall and looks around. He can't find Gus, and he doesn't see the burrow or the old tree. Poor Chase! He is lost. Where should he go?

He needs to get higher. Chase looks out from the top branch of a dry bush. He sees the burrow to the east. As he is about to leave, he spots a lion blocking the way home. What should he do now?

CHAPTER 7

Danger

Chase stands alert. The lion paces back and forth, looking for something to eat.

Lions hunt large animals, such as buffalo or zebra, but in the dry season, they have fewer animals to choose from.

If the lion sees Chase, he might make Chase his next meal. Chase has no choice but to wait for the lion to leave.

Standing as still as he can, Chase waits in the bush. The lion walks closer but stops. Something is coming.

The lion sees something slither across the sand. It's a cape cobra! The lion has not seen Chase yet, but the long yellow snake has.

This is not good! If the mob were here, they would stand together, but Chase is alone. He cannot escape a snake by himself, nor can he fight off a big lion!

As the snake slowly slides around a rock, an eagle cries above. Not only does Chase have a lion and a snake tracking him, but also an eagle!

Chase really needs to get home to the mob. He needs Gus! Gus would know what to do.

At that moment, the eagle dives down from the sky. Oh no! What will happen to Chase?

The eagle spreads his wings, opens his claws, and swoops away from Chase. The long yellow cobra is scooped up by the eagle.

The eagle's loud screech and all the fuss he makes stop the lion in his tracks. He still hasn't seen Chase. Thinking there is nothing left for him to eat, he moves on to hunt somewhere else.

Chase is safe for now.

CHAPTER 8
A Good Rain

Back home, Gus waits for Chase to return. Where could that little pup have gone?

Gus stands tall and looks across the sand.

Gus sees Chase. He also sees a hyena hiding in the bush. Chase runs across the open sand. He doesn't know about the hyena behind him.

Gus barks loudly to alert Chase and the mob. A dozen heads pop up and see the hyena too. The hyena whoops at the meerkats. Chase hears barking and whooping. He is not safe yet.

The meerkats dive into holes. Chase dives into the bolt hole Gus made just in time. The hyena loses again.

No longer in danger, Chase comes out from the bolt hole and runs to his family.

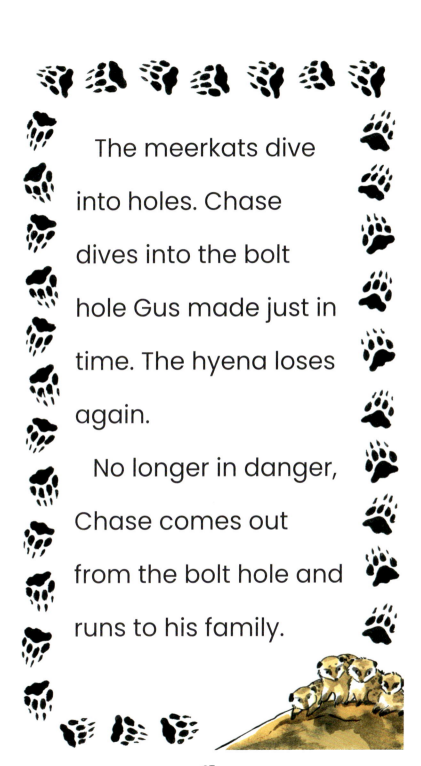

Hank and Penny are glad to have their lost pup home. Penny gives Chase a hug. Chase is glad to see Gus. He has learned his lesson, and he will stay close to Gus from now on.

As Chase joins the other young pups in a game of tag, hundreds of weaver birds flock to the large nest in the old tree. The birds know something big is coming.

A few small raindrops fall from the sky, followed by a burst of big drops. Roxy, Rex, Lola, and Chase romp in the sand. The young pups have never seen or felt rain.

The mob is happy for the rain. All the animals of the Kalahari are thankful for the rain.

Soon water holes fill, and zebra and buffalo return. The dry brown bushes turn green, and yellow flowers bloom across the land. Life returns to the Kalahari.

Check out these other Level 2A books from The Good and the Beautiful!

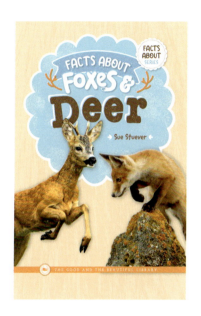

Facts About Foxes and Deer

By Sue Stuever

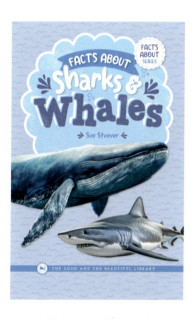

Facts About Sharks and Whales

By Sue Stuever

goodandbeautiful.com

Check out this Level 2B series

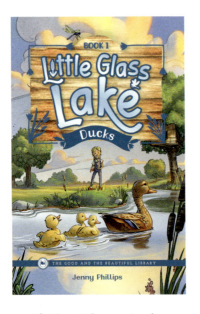

Little Glass Lake: Ducks

By Jenny Phillips

Little Glass Lake: Turtles

By Jenny Phillips

goodandbeautiful.com

from The Good and the Beautiful!

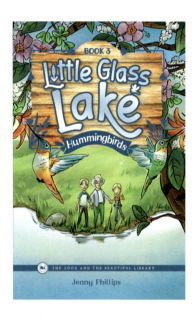

Little Glass Lake: Hummingbirds

By Jenny Phillips

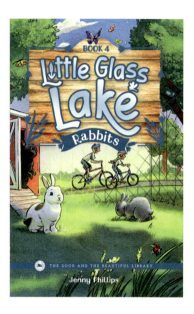

Little Glass Lake: Rabbits

By Jenny Phillips

goodandbeautiful.com